KALEIDOSCOPE

Teeth

Beth Ferguson

***B**ENCHMARK **B**OOKS*

MARSHALL CAVENDISH
NEW YORK

Benchmark Books
Marshall Cavendish
99 White Plains Rd.
Tarrytown, NY 10591
www.marshallcavendish.com

Library of Congress Cataloging-in-Publication Data

Ferguson, Beth, 1968–
  Teeth / by Beth Ferguson.
      v. cm. — (Kaleidoscope)
Contents: Teeth are for chewing — Two sets of teeth — Four kinds of
teeth — The parts of a tooth — When teeth need help — Cavities and
gum disease — Keeping teeth healthy.
  ISBN 0-7614-1589-0
  1. Teeth—Juvenile literature. [1. Teeth.] I. Title. II. Series.

QM311.F47 2004
611'.314—dc21
                    2002155872

Photo research by Anne Burns Images

Cover photo: Photo Researchers: Biophoto Associates/Science Source

The photographs in this book are used by permission and through the courtesy of: *Corbis*: title page; Tom Stewart
Photography, 40; Norbert Schafer, 8; Bill Varie, 20; Peter Beck, 28; Nancy Brown, 35; Thom Lang, 36; Jose Luis Pelaez,
39; Ed Wheeler, 43. *Custom Medical Stock Photo*: 4, 11, 12, 31. *Phototake*: Benedet 7; 15. *Photo Researchers Inc.*:
CNRI/Science Photo Library, 16; Andrew Syred/Science Photo Library 19; Biophoto Associates 23; Bo Veisland,
MI&I/Science Photo Library, 24; Quest/Science Photo Library, 27; John Bavosi/Science Photo Library, 32.

Series design by Adam Mietlowski

Printed in Italy

6 5 4 3 2 1

Contents

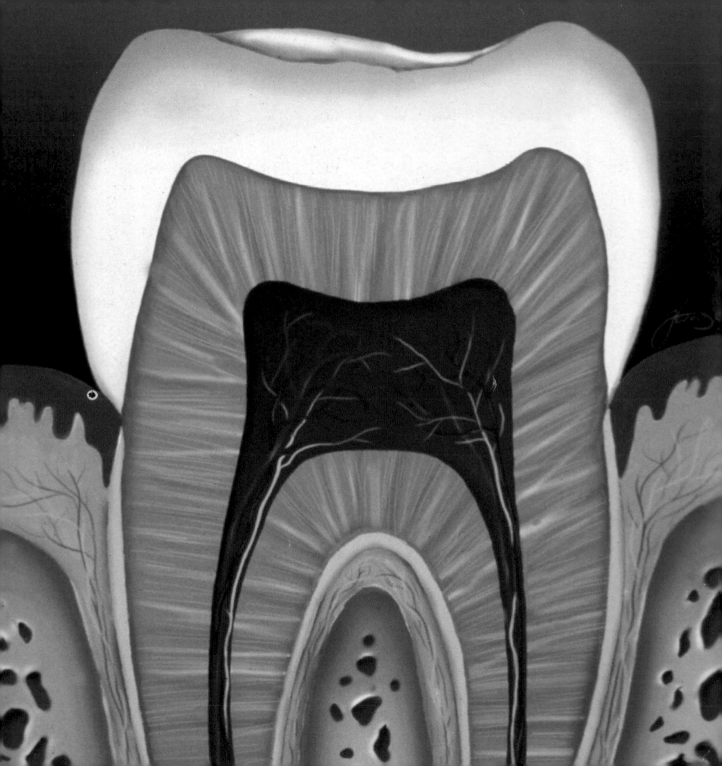

Teeth Are For Chewing

What's the hardest part of your body? It's not your bones or your fingernails. It's your teeth. Teeth need to be strong because they chew up all the food you eat.

When you chew your food, **digestion** begins. During this process, the bits of food you swallow travel to your stomach. Chemicals in your stomach break down the bits into even smaller particles called **nutrients**. Next, the nutrients move into your small intestine, where they enter your **blood vessels**. Your blood then carries the nutrients to the rest of your body, so they can help you breathe, flex muscles, and think during tests.

Teeth do other things as well. They help you talk and give you a bright smile. It's hard to imagine what life would be like if you didn't have teeth.

◀ *A look inside a tooth. Your teeth aid digestion and help your body get the nutrients it needs.*

Two Sets of Teeth

When you were born, you didn't have any teeth in your mouth. But by the time you were about six months old, your first **milk tooth** had appeared. As you continued to grow, more milk teeth popped up one by one. Your front teeth probably came in first, followed by your back teeth. The pointy middle teeth most likely pushed up through your gums last. By your second birthday, you had a mouth full of twenty tiny milk teeth.

Your milk teeth were perfect for eating all kinds of food. But as your body grew, there was more and more extra room inside your mouth. When you were about six years old, you started losing your milk teeth. They were pushed out by larger, more powerful **permanent teeth**.

In this X-ray, you can see a child's milk teeth and the permanent teeth (purple and yellow) that will someday push through the gums.

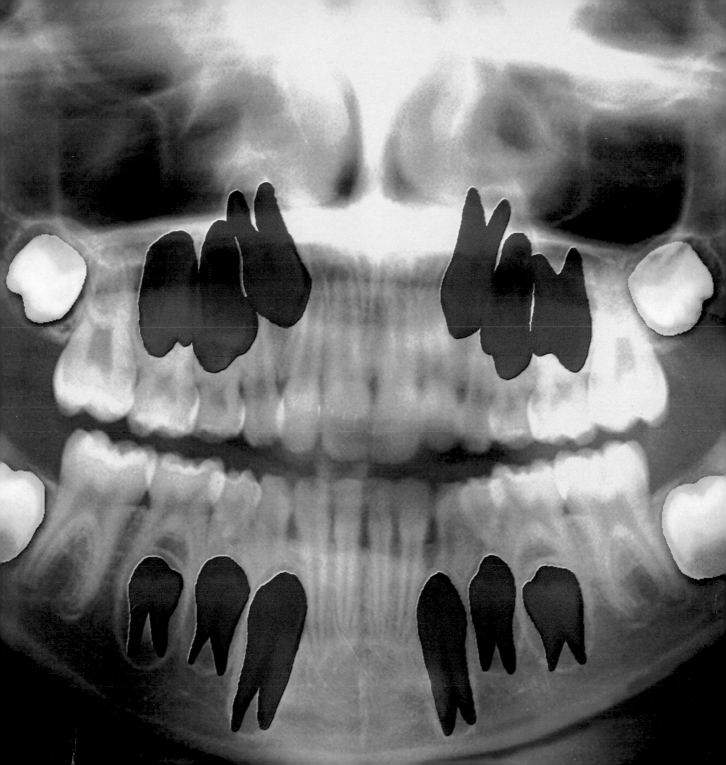

Children lose their milk teeth at different rates. You may have already lost them all, or you may still have a few left. Just about everyone has twenty-eight permanent teeth by his or her twelfth birthday. The last four permanent teeth, called **wisdom teeth**, usually appear by the time a person is twenty-five years old. But some people never get wisdom teeth.

◀ *This girl has lost her front, top milk teeth. Soon, her permanent teeth will move in.*

Four Kinds of Teeth

Take a look at your teeth in a mirror. Teeth come in different sizes and shapes. But the teeth on the right side of your mouth are exactly the same as the teeth on the left side of your mouth. And the teeth on top match the teeth on the bottom, so they fit together when you chew.

The teeth in the front of your mouth are called **incisors**. Small and sharp, they are perfect for cutting through an apple or a carrot. Everyone has eight incisors—four on top and four on the bottom.

This drawing shows a full set of human teeth. The two halves closely match and fit together in your mouth. ▶

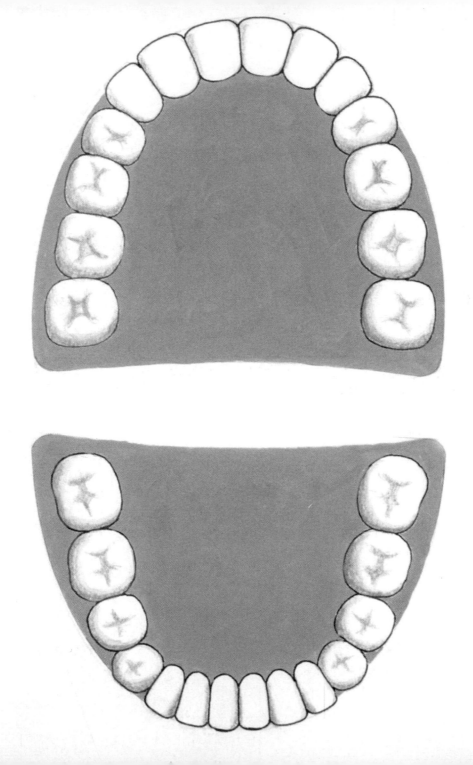

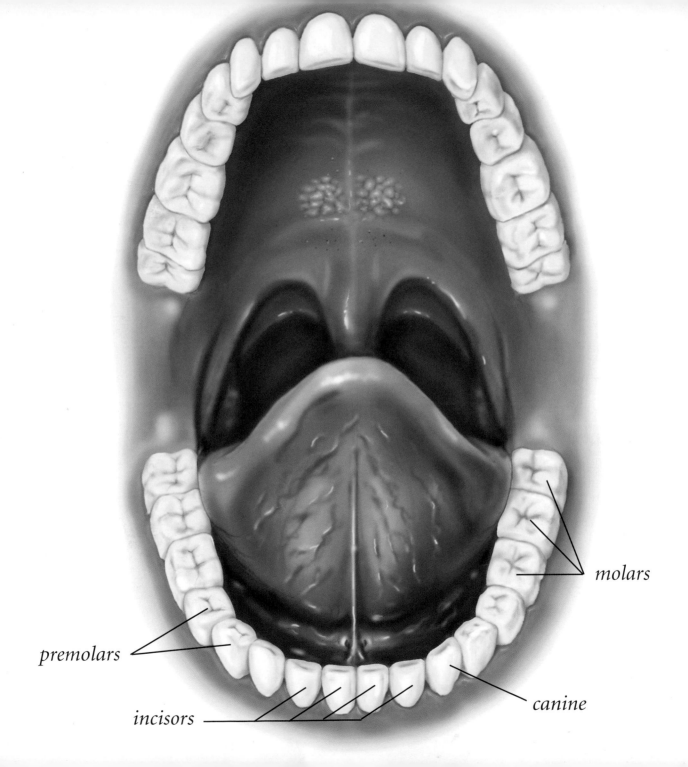

molars

premolars

incisors

canine

Behind your incisors are pointy teeth called **canines**. The word *canine* is Latin for "dog." Canine teeth are similar to the fangs dogs use to rip and chew meat. Like dogs, people use their canine teeth to tear foods. Both children and adults have four canine teeth—two on the top and two on the bottom.

Farther back are the **premolars**. They have two pointy peaks called **cusps** on top. The **molars** are located all the way in the back of your mouth. They are larger and wider than premolars and have three cusps on top. Both the premolars and the molars grind and mash foods. Children with milk teeth have no premolars and eight molars. People with permanent teeth have eight premolars and twelve molars.

The four groups of teeth in your mouth work together to get digestion started. Your incisors and canines grab, cut, and tear foods and bring them into your mouth. Then your premolars and molars chew the food into smaller pieces that can be swallowed.

This drawing of an adult's teeth includes eight incisors, four canines, eight premolars, and twelve molars.

The Parts of a Tooth

Below your bottom teeth and above your top teeth are soft, pink **gums**. Your gums wrap around your **jawbones** and hold your teeth in place. Your upper jawbone is part of your skull, so it cannot move. But your lower jawbone is a separate bone. When you talk or chew, powerful muscles move your lower jawbone up and down and from side to side.

The part of a tooth that extends into your jawbone is called the **root**. It is surrounded by a thin, tough outer layer called **cementum**. Cementum anchors each tooth to your jawbone.

Your gums cover your jawbone and help hold each tooth in place. ▶

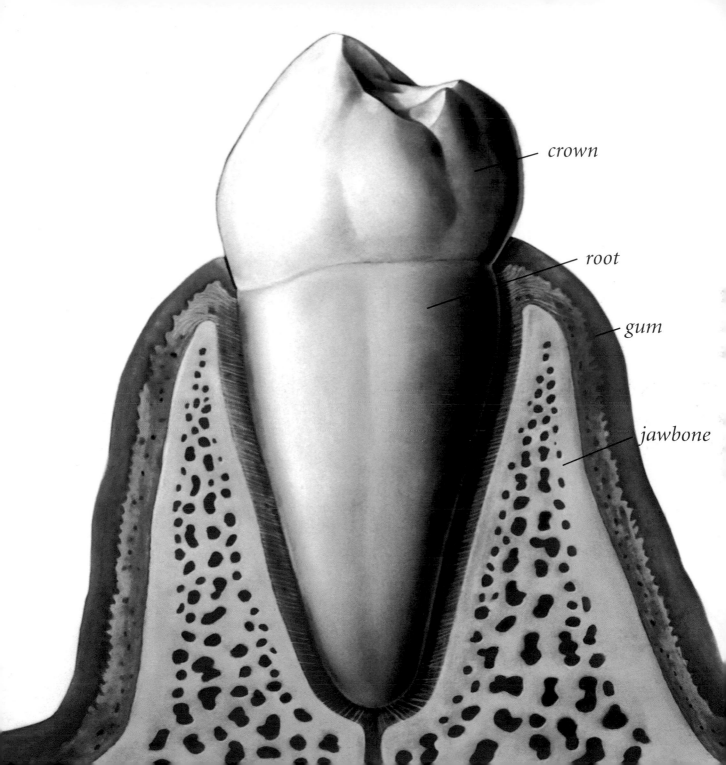

crown

root

gum

jawbone

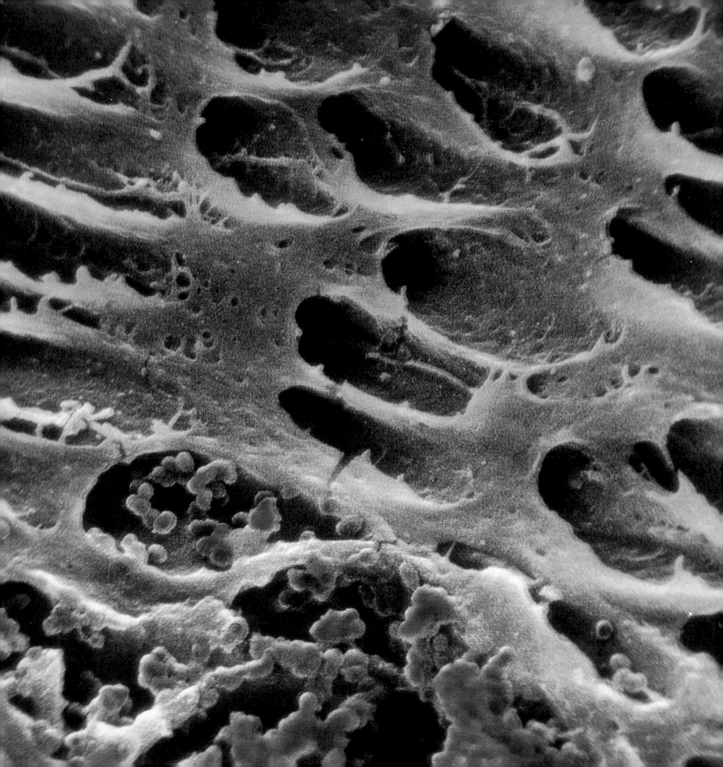

Underneath the cementum is a thick, bonelike layer called **dentin**. Dentin surrounds and protects the tooth's soft central **pulp**. Tiny **nerves** and blood vessels run through the pulp and into your jawbone. The blood vessels carry oxygen and nutrients to the tooth. The nerves sense heat, cold, and pain and send messages to your brain.

◄ *This photo was taken through a high-power microscope. It shows dentin (blue) that is being attacked by bacteria (red).*

When you look at a tooth in a mirror, you see its **crown**. Because the crowns of your teeth do all the biting and chewing, they are made of a very hard material called **enamel**. Enamel protects the softer, inner parts of teeth from harmful **bacteria** and from temperature changes caused by eating hot or cold foods. Over time, coffee, tea, and certain kinds of food can stain the enamel on a person's teeth. That is why most children have pearly white teeth, but many adults have teeth that look slightly yellow.

This photo, which was taken through a high-power microscope, shows the enamel that makes up the crown of the tooth and helps to protect it.

When Teeth Need Help

An elephant can grow as many as six sets of teeth in its lifetime. Sharks and crocodiles can keep on replacing their teeth as long as they live. But humans have only two sets of teeth—milk teeth and permanent teeth. If you break or lose a permanent tooth, a new, healthy tooth will not take its place. That's why it's so important to take care of your teeth everyday.

◄ *A crocodile has a mouth full of sharp teeth. Whenever its teeth are damaged or pulled out, new ones grow in to take their place.*

Even though teeth are very hard, sometimes they crack, chip, or break. Damaged teeth can usually be fixed by a dentist. In some cases, the dentist will cap an injured tooth. This involves placing an artificial crown over the damaged tooth and gluing it in place. Most of the time, an artificial crown looks and works just like the original tooth.

If a tooth is missing or needs to be pulled, a dentist may replace it with a false tooth that is held in place by a **bridge**. The bridge attaches the false tooth to healthy teeth on either side. In some cases, dentists replace a lost tooth with an **implant**—a false tooth that is permanently attached to the jawbone. Sometimes a person is missing so many teeth that a bridge won't work and implants would cost too much money. Then the dentist may pull all of the remaining teeth and give the person **dentures**, a complete set of false teeth.

This person has had a lot of dental work. Notice the two gold crowns (bottom left and right) over the molars at the back of the mouth.

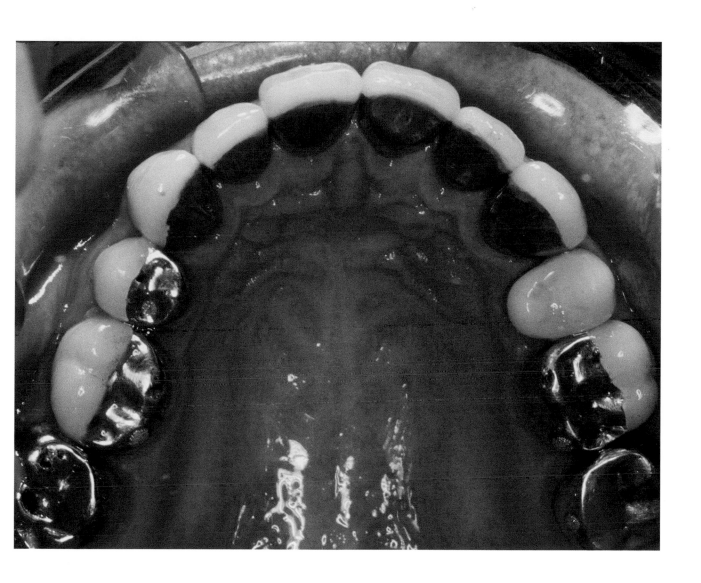

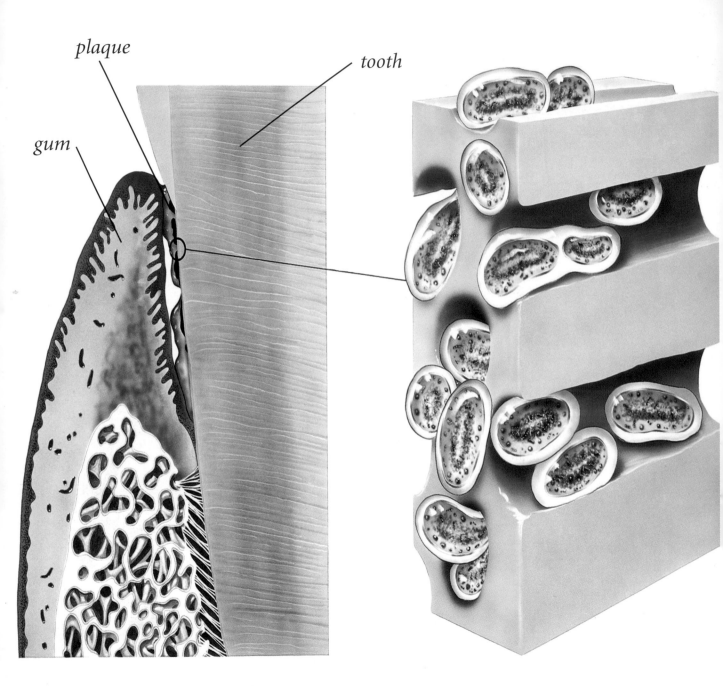

Cavities and Gum Disease

Even if you do not lose or damage your teeth, you may still have some trouble with them. The most common problem affecting teeth is **tooth decay**. It is caused by bacteria that live in your mouth. As the bacteria grow, they make a harmful acid that attacks and slowly breaks down or eats away at your teeth.

◀ *The drawing on the left shows a layer of plaque lodged between a person's gums and tooth. The drawing on the right shows a close-up view of bacteria eating away at a person's tooth.*

Most of the food you eat ends up in your stomach, but a few small bits get caught in or between your teeth. Bacteria are small enough to fit into these spaces and feast on the leftovers. As the bacteria feed, they grow and divide rapidly. Eventually, a soft, sticky film called plaque forms on your teeth and along your gums. If you do not brush your teeth thoroughly, these patches of **plaque** will harden into **tartar**. Once tartar has formed, it is hard to remove from your teeth.

This photo, which was taken through a high-power microscope, shows plaque on a person's tooth. How many different kinds of bacteria can you see? ▶

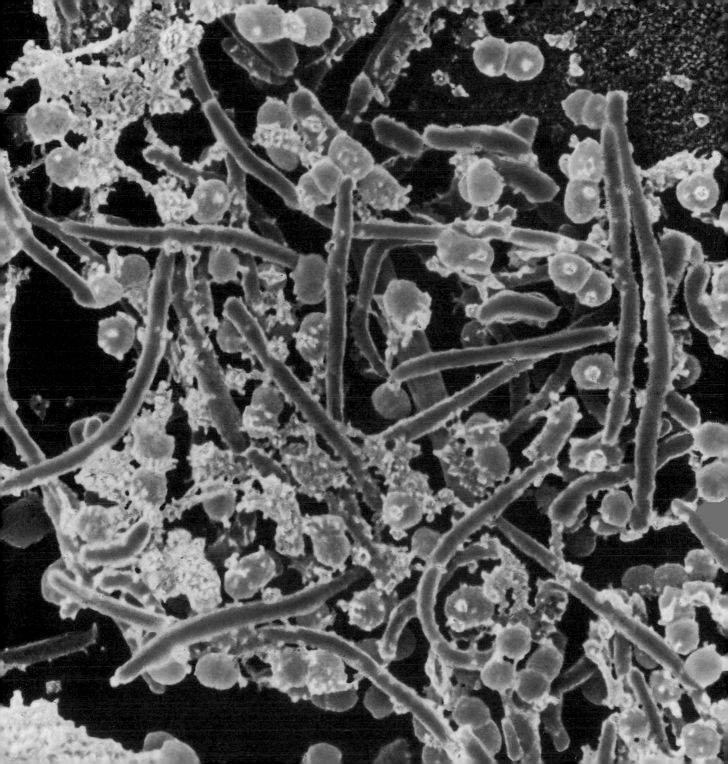

Sugar from the foods you eat sticks to plaque and tartar. This attracts more bacteria and causes even more tooth decay. Eventually, the decay will spread through your tooth's crown and into the dentin. The resulting hole is called a **cavity**. Unless a dentist notices the cavity, it will grow bigger and deeper. Over time, bacteria may eat all the way through the dentin to your tooth's soft pulp.

Some people get cavities more easily than others, but nearly everyone has experienced some tooth decay by the time he or she is fourteen years old. Most cavities form in the deep grooves along molars.

This dentist is showing a girl an X-ray of her teeth. It reveals that she has a cavity.

When a dentist finds a cavity, he or she uses a drill or a high-speed stream of air to clean out the hole. If the cavity is in a back tooth, the dentist will fill it with **amalgam**, a mixture of silver and other metals. If the cavity is in a front tooth, the dentist may use porcelain instead. Because porcelain is white, this kind of filling blends in with the rest of the tooth.

If bacteria have eaten all the way into the soft pulp layer of a tooth, a dentist may have to remove the infected pulp from the **root canal**. He or she then replaces it with a special material that helps hold the tooth in place.

The root of a tooth is another area where problems can occur. This drawing shows an infection where the root tip meets the nerve. ▶

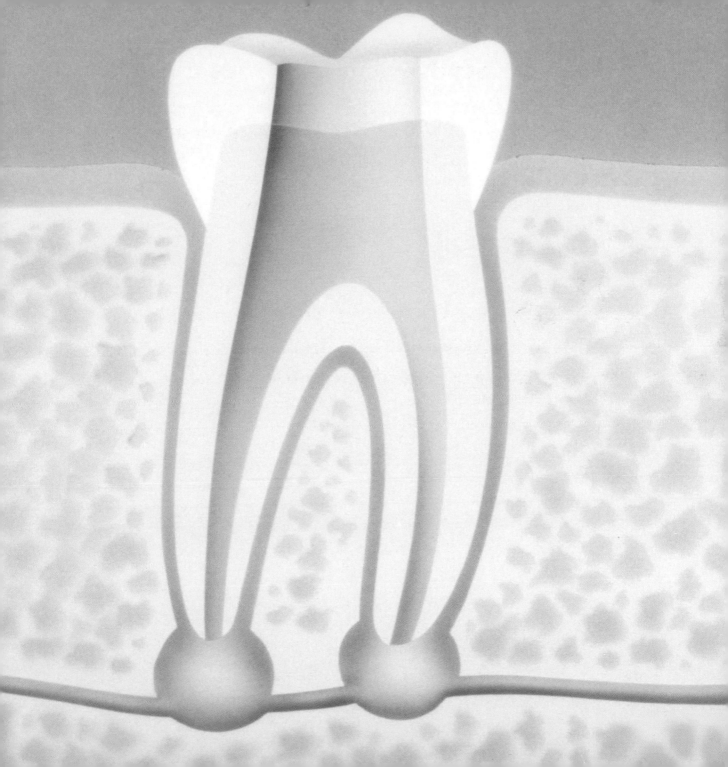

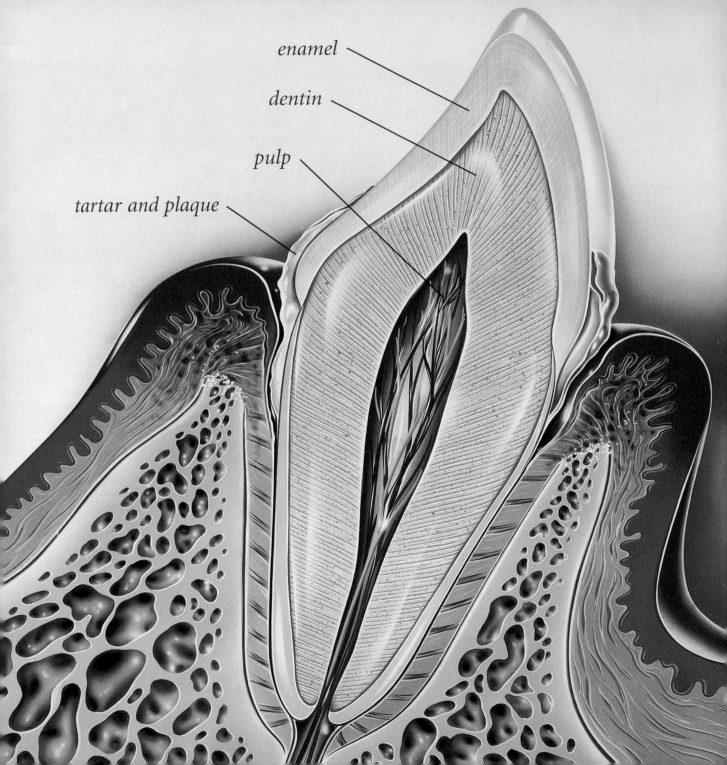

enamel

dentin

pulp

tartar and plaque

Sometimes bacteria grow down into a person's gums and cause **gum disease**. Gum disease is much more common in adults than in children. As bacteria attack gum tissue, the gums begin to pull away from a person's teeth. This leaves a space between the teeth and gums, where even more bacteria can live.

People with a kind of gum disease called **gingivitis** have red, swollen gums that bleed easily. Most of the time, gingivitis can be cured by brushing more gently and thoroughly. However, if gingivitis is not treated, the disease may become more serious. Eventually, the bacteria will begin to attack a person's jawbone. Then a dentist may have to remove the infected part of the gum so the bacteria will stop spreading.

◄ *This drawing shows the tooth and gums of a person with gum disease. You can see that the gums are swollen and have begun to pull away from the person's tooth.*

Brushing and flossing every day can help prevent cavities and gum disease. But if a person's teeth are crowded, crooked, or do not line up properly, it may be hard to keep them clean. If this is the case, your dentist may send you to an **orthodontist**. The orthodontist may pull a few teeth so the others have room to spread out. He or she may also recommend **braces** to straighten your teeth.

Over time, this boy's braces will straighten his teeth. ▶

Keeping Teeth Healthy

Only a dental professional can straighten crooked teeth, fill cavities, or replace lost teeth. But there are plenty of simple things you can do to keep your teeth healthy.

A good place to start is at the dinner table. Be sure to drink plenty of milk and eat cheese, yogurt, green leafy vegetables, and fruit. These foods are good sources of calcium, phosphorus, and vitamins D and C. They help keep your teeth healthy and strong.

Try to avoid candy, gum, cookies, granola bars, raisins and other sticky or sugary foods. Also be careful when you eat potato chips and crackers. These snack foods may not taste sweet, but they form sugars when they mix with saliva. Over time, those sugars will attract bacteria.

Cherries are just one of the many foods that provide the vitamins your body needs to keep teeth healthy.

When you do eat these foods, brush your teeth as soon as you are done. Brushing not only removes food particles and plaque, it also freshens your breath. If you can't brush, at least rinse your mouth with water. Cleaning your teeth and gums after every meal and snack is the best way to guarantee a healthy smile.

If you brush and floss your teeth every day, good dental care will become a habit. When you brush, gently move your toothbrush up and down and in circles along your teeth and gums. As you brush your top teeth, move your toothbrush downward from your gums. As you brush your bottom teeth, move your toothbrush upward from your gums. Don't forget the back of your teeth! Be sure to use a toothpaste with fluoride and a soft-bristled toothbrush that is the right size for your mouth. Ask your dentist what kind of toothbrush would be best for you, and then remember to replace it every three months.

If you brush regularly, you will have healthy teeth and fresh breath. ▶

You should floss at least once a day. Flossing removes plaque that forms between teeth and along the gumline. These are places your toothbrush cannot reach. When you floss, insert the floss between two teeth and gently pull it back and forth along the edges of your teeth and gums.

◄ *Flossing cleans areas of your teeth and gums that your toothbrush cannot reach.*

Sometimes brushing and flossing are not enough to keep your teeth healthy. That's why you should visit a dentist twice a year. Your dentist will check for signs of tooth decay and clean your teeth with special equipment. He or she may also apply fluoride to your teeth or coat them with a sealant. These treatments will make your teeth stronger and give you extra protection against bacteria. By listening to and working with your dentist, you can have a healthy smile that will last you a lifetime.

When it comes to keeping your teeth clean and healthy, your dentist is your best friend.

▶

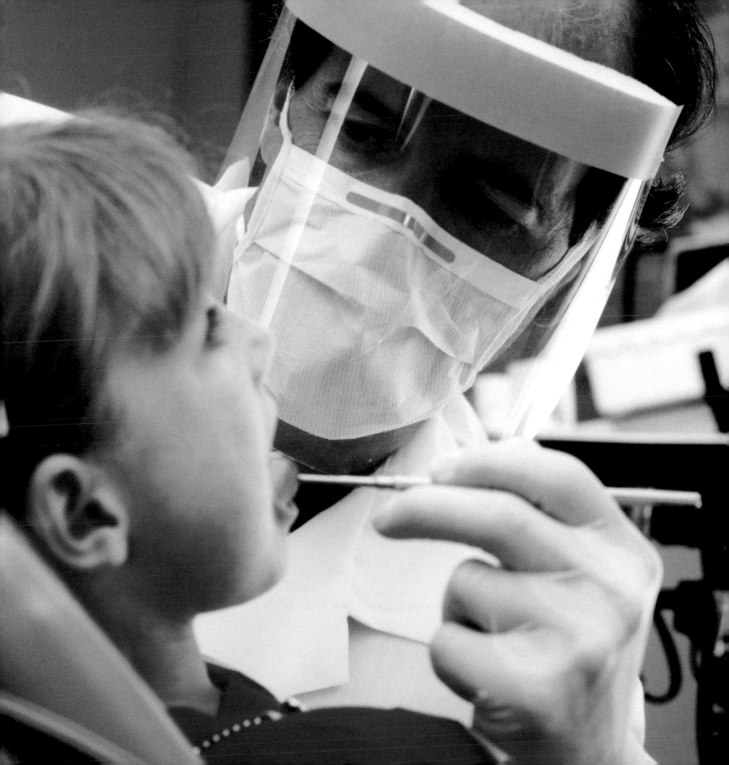

Glossary

amalgam—A mixture of silver and other materials that is often used to fill cavities in teeth.

bacterium (pl. bacteria)—A tiny, one-celled living thing that reproduces by dividing.

blood vessel—One of the tiny tubes that carries blood through the body.

braces—Dental equipment used to straighten or move teeth.

bridge—A dental device that connects a false tooth to surrounding healthy teeth.

canine—One of the pointed teeth behind the incisors. Canine teeth are used to tear foods.

cavity—A hole in a tooth caused by tooth decay.

cementum—The outermost layer of the root of a tooth. It attaches the tooth to the gums and jawbone.

crown—The part of a tooth above the gumline.

cusp—A small pointy peak along the top of a molar or premolar.

dentin—A hard, bony material that makes up most of a tooth. It protects the pulp.

dentures—A set of false teeth that can be removed and then put back in.

digestion—The process by which the human body breaks down food and absorbs nutrients.

enamel—The hard outermost layer of the crown of a tooth.

gingivitis—A kind of gum disease that causes redness and swelling.

gum disease—Damage to the gums caused by bacteria.

gums—The soft pink tissue that wraps around the bottoms of teeth and holds them in place.

implant—A false tooth that is permanently attached to the jawbone.

incisor—One of the front teeth that cuts through hard foods, such as apples and carrots.

jawbone—One of the bones to which teeth are attached. The upper jawbone is part of the skull, but the lower jaw is separate and can move.

milk teeth—A child's first set of teeth.

molar—One of the large wide teeth at the back of a person's mouth. Molars are used to mash and grind foods.

nerve—A cell or group of cells that sends messages to the brain.

nutrient—A substance used to keep the body healthy.

orthodontist—A dental professional who treats patients with teeth that are crooked, crowded, or do not line up properly.

permanent teeth—Teeth that replace milk teeth.

plaque—A mixture of leftover food bits, bacteria, and other materials.

premolar—One of the teeth in front of the molars, but behind the canines. Premolars are used to mash and grind foods.

pulp—The soft, central part of a tooth that contains nerves and blood vessels.

root—The part of the tooth below the gumline.

root canal—The portion of the pulp below the gumline.

tartar—Hardened plaque.

tooth decay—Damage caused by bacteria that release an acid that eats away at teeth.

wisdom tooth—One of the four molars in the back of the mouth. Some people never get wisdom teeth. Other people need to have them pulled so their other teeth are not too crowded.

Find Out More

Books

Beeler, Selby B. *Throw Your Tooth on the Roof: Tooth Traditions from Around the World.* New York: Boston, 1998.

Keller, Laurie. *Open Wide: Tooth School Inside.* New York: Henry Holt, 2000.

Rowan, Kate. *I Know Why I Brush My Teeth.* Cambridge, MA: Candlewick Press, 1999.

Silverstein, Alvin, Virginia Silverstein, and Laura Silverstein Nunn. *Tooth Decay and Cavities.* Danbury, CT: Franklin Watts, 2000.

Sis, Peter. *Madlenka.* New York: Frances Foster Books, 2000.

Organizations and Online Sites

American Dental Association
211 East Chicago Ave.
Chicago, IL 60611
www.ada.org
ADA "Kids Corner" with coloring sheets and movies
http://www.ada.org/public/topics/kids/index.html

Clean Teeth and Gums

www.pe.net/~iddpc1/clean.htm

Having a clean mouth is important. In addition to being healthier, it gives you fresh breath and a nicer smile. To learn more about brushing and flossing, go to this Web site.

Diet and Dental Health

www.pe.net/~iddpc1/diet.htm

You know that what you eat can make a difference in the way you feel and perform. But did you know that your choice of foods can affect your teeth? Check out this site for more information.

Author's Bio

Beth Ferguson earned a bachelor's degree in biology from Union College and a master's degree in science and environmental journalism from New York University. After working as an editor for many years, she now writes about science and medicine. Ms. Ferguson lives in Massachusetts.

Index